PLANET

UNDER

PRESSURE

WELBECK

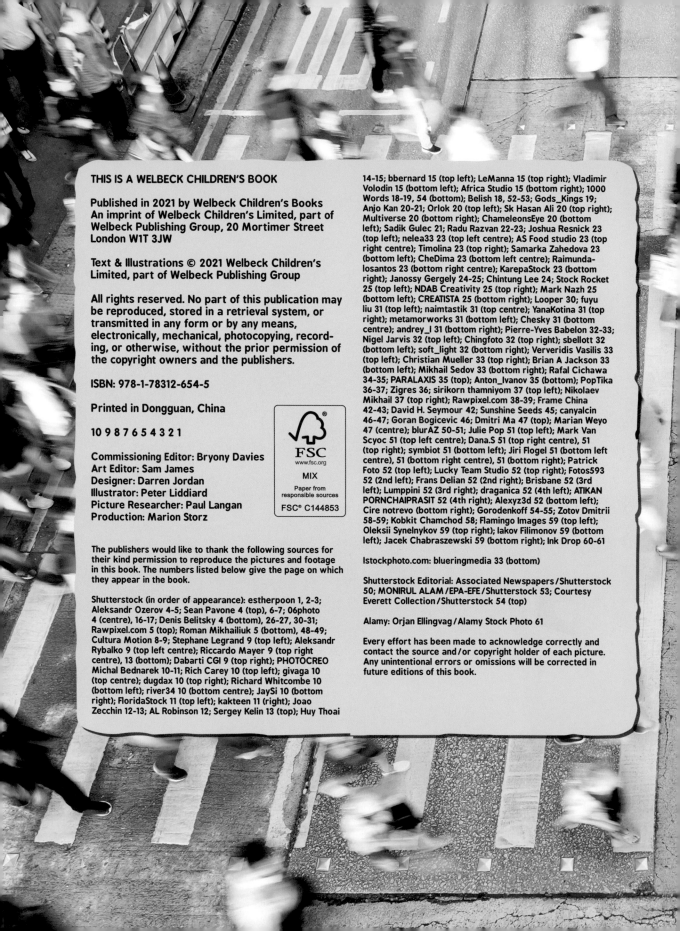

THIS IS A WELBECK CHILDREN'S BOOK

Published in 2021 by Welbeck Children's Books
An imprint of Welbeck Children's Limited, part of
Welbeck Publishing Group, 20 Mortimer Street
London W1T 3JW

ISBN: 978-1-78312-654-5

Printed in Dongguan, China

10 9 8 7 6 5 4 3 2 1

Commissioning Editor: Bryony Davies
Art Editor: Sam James
Designer: Darren Jordan
Illustrator: Peter Liddiard
Picture Researcher: Paul Langan
Production: Marion Storz

FSC
www.fsc.org
MIX
Paper from
responsible sources
FSC® C144853

The publishers would like to thank the following sources for
their kind permission to reproduce the pictures and footage
in this book. The numbers listed below give the page on which
they appear in the book.

Shutterstock (in order of appearance): estherpoon 1, 2-3;
Aleksandr Ozerov 4-5; Sean Pavone 4 (top), 6-7; 06photo
4 (centre), 16-17; Denis Belitsky 4 (bottom), 26-27, 30-31;
Rawpixel.com 5 (top); Roman Mikhailiuk 5 (bottom), 48-49;
Cultura Motion 8-9; Stephane Legrand 9 (top left); Aleksandr
Rybalko 9 (top left centre); Riccardo Mayer 9 (top right
centre), 13 (bottom); Dabarti CGI 9 (top right); PHOTOCREO
Michal Bednarek 10-11; Rich Carey 10 (top left); givaga 10
(top centre); dugdax 10 (top right); Richard Whitcombe 10
(bottom left); river34 10 (bottom centre); JaySi 10 (bottom
right); FloridaStock 11 (top left); kakteen 11 (right); Joao
Zecchin 12-13; AL Robinson 12; Sergey Kelin 13 (top); Huy Thoai
14-15; bbernard 15 (top left); LeManna 15 (top right); Vladimir
Volodin 15 (bottom left); Africa Studio 15 (bottom right); 1000
Words 18-19, 54 (bottom); Belish 18, 52-53; Gods_Kings 19;
Anjo Kan 20-21; Orlok 20 (top left); Sk Hasan Ali 20 (top right);
Multiverse 20 (bottom right); ChameleonsEye 20 (bottom
left); Sadik Gulec 21; Radu Razvan 22-23; Joshua Resnick 23
(top left); nelea33 23 (top left centre); AS Food studio 23 (top
right centre); Timolina 23 (top right); Samarka Zahedova 23
(bottom left); CheDima 23 (bottom left centre); Raimunda-
losantos 23 (bottom right centre); KarepaStock 23 (bottom
right); Janossy Gergely 24-25; Chintung Lee 24; Stock Rocket
25 (top left); NDAB Creativity 25 (top right); Mark Nazh 25
(bottom left); CREATISTA 25 (bottom right); Looper 30; fuyu
liu 31 (top left); naimtastik 31 (top centre); YanaKotina 31 (top
right); metamorworks 31 (bottom left); Chesky 31 (bottom
centre); andrey_l 31 (bottom right); Pierre-Yves Babelon 32-33;
Nigel Jarvis 32 (top left); Chingfoto 32 (top right); sbellott 32
(bottom left); soft_light 32 (bottom right); Ververidis Vasilis 33
(top left); Christian Mueller 33 (top right); Brian A Jackson 33
(bottom left); Mikhail Sedov 33 (bottom right); Rafal Cichawa
34-35; PARALAXIS 35 (top); Anton_Ivanov 35 (bottom); PopTika
36-37; Zigres 36; sirikorn thamniyom 37 (top left); Nikolaev
Mikhail 37 (top right); Rawpixel.com 38-39; Frame China
42-43; David H. Seymour 42; Sunshine Seeds 45; canyalcin
46-47; Goran Bogicevic 46; Dmitri Ma 47 (top); Marian Weyo
47 (centre); blurAZ 50-51; Julie Pop 51 (top left); Mark Van
Scyoc 51 (top left centre); Dana.S 51 (top right centre), 51
(top right); symbiot 51 (bottom left); Jiri Flogel 51 (bottom left
centre), 51 (bottom right centre), 51 (bottom right); Patrick
Foto 52 (top left); Lucky Team Studio 52 (top right); Fotos593
52 (2nd left); Frans Delian 52 (2nd right); Brisbane 52 (3rd
left); Lumppini 52 (3rd right); draganica 52 (4th left); ATIKAN
PORNCHAIPRASIT 52 (4th right); Alexyz3d 52 (bottom left);
Cire notrevo (bottom right); Gorodenkoff 54-55; Zotov Dmitrii
58-59; Kobkit Chamchod 58; Flamingo Images 59 (top left);
Oleksii Synelnykov 59 (top right); Iakov Filimonov 59 (bottom
left); Jacek Chabraszewski 59 (bottom right); Ink Drop 60-61

Istockphoto.com: blueringmedia 33 (bottom)

Shutterstock Editorial: Associated Newspapers/Shutterstock
50; MONIRUL ALAM/EPA-EFE/Shutterstock 53; Courtesy
Everett Collection/Shutterstock 54 (top)

Alamy: Orjan Ellingvag/Alamy Stock Photo 61

Every effort has been made to acknowledge correctly and
contact the source and/or copyright holder of each picture.
Any unintentional errors or omissions will be corrected in
future editions of this book.

PLANET UNDER PRESSURE

Written by Nancy Dickmann

WELBECK

CONTENTS

PEOPLE, PEOPLE EVERYWHERE

Sometimes it seems as though there are people everywhere you look. Cities, stores, restaurants, and museums are crowded with people. Even large public parks fill up on a nice day! There are more people living on Earth than ever before. The population has increased enormously over the centuries, and it will continue to grow.

POPULATION CHALLENGES

Population growth has led to many changes. People are living in parts of Earth that used to be wild. We have built cities and skyscrapers, squeezing ever more people onto the same amount of land. Our growing population has led to many challenges that are set to grow in the future, such as increased pressure on the world's resources, climate change, and habitat destruction.

POPULATION PRESSURE

Around the year AD 100 there were probably about 200 million people in the world. Even a thousand years ago, there were only about 300 million. Historians think that Earth's population hit 1 billion for the first time around 1800. Since then it has skyrocketed! Today there are almost 8 billion people on the planet.

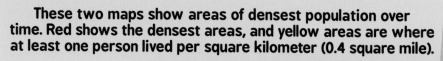

These two maps show areas of densest population over time. Red shows the densest areas, and yellow areas are where at least one person lived per square kilometer (0.4 square mile).

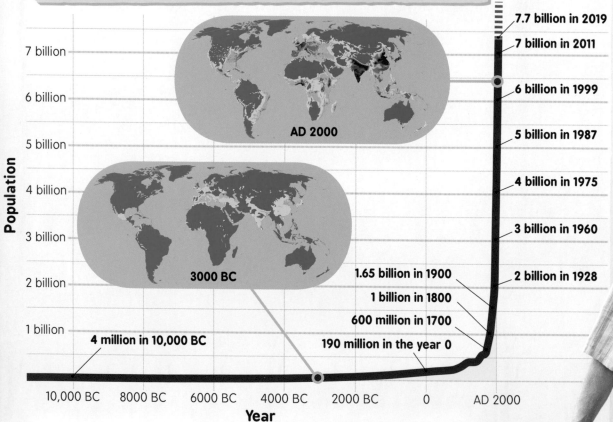

Population

7 billion
6 billion
5 billion
4 billion
3 billion
2 billion
1 billion

AD 2000

3000 BC

4 million in 10,000 BC

1.65 billion in 1900
1 billion in 1800
600 million in 1700
190 million in the year 0

7.7 billion in 2019
7 billion in 2011
6 billion in 1999
5 billion in 1987
4 billion in 1975
3 billion in 1960
2 billion in 1928

10,000 BC 8000 BC 6000 BC 4000 BC 2000 BC 0 AD 2000

Year

LIVING LONGER

The main reason for the recent population growth is that people are living longer. Thanks to better medical care, we can fight and prevent more dangerous diseases. In 1800 about 45 percent of children died before the age of five. People's average life expectancy was less than 30 years. Today it's more than 70.

USING RESOURCES

A large population puts a huge amount of pressure on Earth's resources.

LAND

Homes gobble up land that used to be wild.

FOOD

Farmers need to use land to grow more food.

WATER

A limited supply of fresh water must be shared by more people.

FUEL

Modern lifestyles require more fuel.

HOW HIGH CAN WE GO?

Scientists make predictions about what Earth's population will be in the future. People are having fewer children than in the past, but more children survive today, and they live longer. Here is one estimate of Earth's future population.

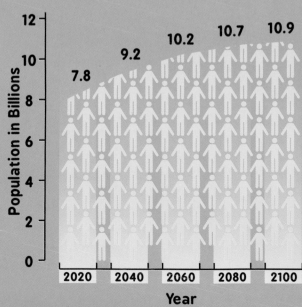

Population in Billions

Year	Population
2020	7.8
2040	9.2
2060	10.2
2080	10.7
2100	10.9

WHOSE PLANET IS IT?

Humans aren't the only living things on our planet. In fact, we're vastly outnumbered! Everywhere you look, there are animals and plants. There are even tiny creatures and bacteria that are too small to see. This planet belongs to them as well.

Each living thing inhabits its own particular environment, called a habitat. Special features make creatures suited to their habitat. For example, camels' wide, flat hooves walk well on desert sand, and their long lashes keep sand out of their eyes. These are some of the most common habitats.

OCEANS

DESERTS

FORESTS

RAIN FORESTS

POLAR REGIONS

GRASSLANDS

A WARMING PLANET

Our modern lifestyle produces increasing amounts of greenhouse gases, which cause climate change. Earth's temperature is rising, so severe weather is becoming more common. Rising temperatures melt the sea ice that polar bears depend on. Warmer waters damage coral reefs. Hurricanes can uproot trees and destroy coastal habitats.

FORCED OUT

Humans often take over land that is home to plants and animals. We cut down forests to build houses or raise livestock. We plow grasslands to grow crops. We dig for resources below the ground. When this happens, the animals who live there are forced out. Many of the plants are killed.

FACT

Every minute of every day, an area of tropical rain forest approximately the size of 43 football fields is destroyed.

TOTALLY TRUE - OR - FOOLISHLY FALSE?

A. For every person living on Earth, there are almost 200 trees.

B. There are about 6,400 different species of mammals.

C. About 10,000 plant and animal species are listed as "threatened," meaning they are at risk of extinction.

Find the answers at the back of the book.

RICH AND POOR

In an ideal world, Earth's resources would be shared equally. But the sad truth is that they aren't. Many people live a comfortable life, with everything they need. Others scrape by, with little money for luxuries. And many people live in poverty, facing a daily challenge to survive.

CITIES AND SLUMS

It's not a question of rich people living in one part of the world and poor people living in another. In many places, they live side by side. In big cities such as London, England, or São Paulo, Brazil, the rich live in large, comfortable homes while poor residents crowd into small, cramped apartment buildings. Some even live in homemade shacks or on the streets.

IS THERE ENOUGH FOR EVERYONE?

Almost 11 percent of people in the world don't get enough to eat. Is that because farmers don't produce enough food for everyone? Scientists don't think so. Huge amounts of food are wasted, either during production or by the people who buy it—sometimes as much as one-third of the total supply. And what's left doesn't get divided up equally. If it did, scientists estimate that everyone on the planet would have enough to eat.

BRIDGING THE GAP

Charities work to help the world's poorer population by improving their living standards. They dig wells, build sanitation facilities, and provide vaccinations and other medical care. Some charities train local teachers and other important workers, and some provide loans and grants for people to set up their own businesses.

WHAT'S THE LIMIT?

How many people can Earth support? The rate at which Earth's population is growing is actually now slowing, but the total number of people is still going up. Will we ever reach a point where there just isn't enough to go around?

THINK ABOUT IT!

Better medical care enables people to live longer and longer. How do you think this affects the world's population?

Some countries have made laws limiting the number of children people can have. This is to keep the population from rising too quickly. Do you think this is fair, or should people be allowed to make their own choices?

People in richer countries tend to use up more resources. They travel more, eat more, and buy more. How can we reduce our impact on the planet?

Building places for people to live in often means that natural habitats are destroyed. What are the effects of this? How can we change the way we live to protect plants and animals?

ACTIVITIES TO TRY

WASTE WATCHER
Does your family waste food? To reduce waste, plan meals before you shop and think of creative ways to use up leftovers.

REDUCE YOUR IMPACT
Think about the resources you use, such as energy and plastic. Could you cut down?

FAMILY DETECTIVE
Research your family tree and look back through the generations. Were families bigger in the past?

FUNDRAISING HERO
Raise money for an organization that helps the world's poorest people. You could host a bake sale or do a sponsored challenge.

ARE YOU A POPULATION EXPERT?

Test your knowledge . . .

1. How many people are there on Earth today?

- **A.** Almost 6 billion
- **B.** Almost 8 billion
- **C.** Almost 10 billion

Find the answers at the back of the book.

2. What is the main reason why people live longer today than in the past?

- **A.** They eat more food
- **B.** They wear warmer clothes
- **C.** They get better medical care

3. Why do people cut down rain forests?

- **A.** To use the land for farming
- **B.** To help fight climate change
- **C.** Because they don't like the way they look

PEOPLE ON THE MOVE

The first humans evolved in Africa hundreds of thousands of years ago. Since then we have spread across the planet. People moved in search of new and better sources of food. Eventually, they settled into cities and towns.

In the past, people often lived in the same place for generations. Many of them still do! But others are on the move, sometimes to a different country. This is called migration. People migrate for many reasons. Some choose to work or study somewhere new. Others move for safety and security. They may be fleeing war or natural disasters.

ECONOMIC MIGRATION

Millions of people move from one country to another. Some stay for just a short time. Others settle permanently in their new home. Many of these people move for the same reason: to find better work and a better life.

LOOKING FOR WORK

People who come to a country to work are economic migrants. They hope to earn higher wages and improve their standard of living. Some economic migrants bring their families with them. Others come alone. Many send part of their income home to support their families.

WORK FOR MIGRANTS

Some economic migrants are highly skilled—they might be doctors or specialists in banking or technology. However, it can take time for their qualifications to be recognized in their new countries, and they may have to take classes or pass exams. Other economic migrants work in lower-skilled jobs, such as in factories, stores, hotels, and restaurants.

A FAIR DEAL?

Most economic migrants worldwide have permission to move to the country they choose. They're needed in the workforce and are treated fairly. But some come without permission. Employers can illegally take unfair advantage of these workers. They may pay them less or force them to work long hours. These employees are less likely to complain because they know they risk being sent back home.

FACT

About 272 million people in the world today have migrated to a different country from the one where they were born. That's 3.5 percent of the world's population!

REFUGEES

Economic migrants leave their homes in search of a better life. They have made this choice freely, and they could stay at home if they wanted to. Refugees are different. They are forced to flee their homes.

FORCED OUT

There are many different reasons why people may be forced to leave their homes. These are some of the main reasons:

WAR

Fighting can put ordinary people in danger. This includes wars between countries and within a single country.

PERSECUTION

Some people face persecution because of their religion, ethnic group, sexuality, or political views.

NATURAL DISASTERS

Catastrophic events, such as earthquakes and hurricanes, can destroy homes, farms, and livelihoods.

CLIMATE CHANGE

Earth's changing climate is making some areas hard to live in. Some Pacific islands have already disappeared beneath rising sea levels.

DANGEROUS JOURNEYS

There are about 70 million refugees in the world. Many of them live in poor conditions in large camps, waiting for the chance to go back home or to set up a new life somewhere safe. Some refugees go on dangerous journeys in search of a safer place to live. Thousands have drowned while trying to cross the sea in small, overcrowded boats.

FACT

A civil war broke out in Syria in 2011, putting ordinary people's lives at risk. Since then, more than 5.6 million people have fled.

REFUGEE RIGHTS

The United Nations has set guidelines to help countries treat refugees fairly. The guidelines state that a refugee has the right to be safe, so they should not be sent back home if that would put their life in danger. A refugee also has the right to make the case that they should be admitted to live in another country.

SHARING CULTURES

The world is a mix of many different cultures. As people move around the planet more than ever before, they take their cultures with them. This is making the world more vibrant and diverse. People often come together to celebrate festivals with neighbors from other cultures.

STICKING TOGETHER

Early immigrants often tended to stick together. They would settle in the same neighborhoods, among people who shared their language and culture. This doesn't happen as much today, but many cities still have a "Chinatown" or a "Little Italy."

FITTING IN

Although people have moved around since ancient times, most people in the past stayed within their own local group. People from other places were usually seen as rare and exotic. They were sometimes viewed with suspicion.

SHARING FOOD

People today eat a huge range of dishes. Some of them are so familiar that we forget they originally came from different countries!

TACOS

from Mexico

CURRY

from India

STIR-FRY

from China

PASTA

from Italy

FALAFEL

from the Middle East

PHO

from Vietnam

PAELLA

from Spain

SUSHI

from Japan

MAKING MUSIC

From rock and roll and bhangra to K-pop and steel drums, we're exposed to music from a range of different cultures. One study showed that people were more likely to have a positive view of another culture when they saw one of its members performing music.

TOTALLY TRUE - OR - FOOLISHLY FALSE?

A. Chinese New Year is held on March 15 each year.

B. Diwali is a festival celebrated by Hindus around October or November.

Find the answers at the back of the book.

SHOULD MOVEMENT BE FREE?

Each country makes its own rules about who can come to live in it. In some areas, such as within the European Union (EU), citizens can live and work in any member country. This is called "free movement"—but not everyone thinks it's a good idea.

THINK ABOUT IT!

? Did your family once live somewhere else? How would your life be different if you hadn't migrated? If everyone could live wherever they liked, do you think the world would change?

? In some countries, people pay higher taxes so that services like education and health care can be provided to everyone by the government. Do you think this might make more people want to live there?

? Countries have different ways of deciding who is allowed to live in them. To move to some countries, you might need to have received a job offer. Some countries let you join a relative who is already living in them. What is the fairest way to decide?

STAT MASTER

Do some research online to find out how many people immigrated to your country in the past year. Where did they come from?

SUPER CHEF

Share a recipe from your culture with a friend who's never tried it before. What do they think of it?

HELPING HAND

Find a local charity that helps refugees. What do they need most? You may be able to donate your time, money, or even old clothes.

LANGUAGE LEARNER

How many countries are represented by children at your school? Choose a country and see if you can learn some words or phrases from that nation.

ARE YOU A MIGRATION MASTER?

Test your knowledge . . .

1. What percentage of the world's population lives in a different country from the one where they were born?

- **A.** 1.5 percent
- **B.** 3.5 percent
- **C.** 10 percent

2. Why have millions of people left Syria in recent years?

- **A.** They were fleeing civil war
- **B.** An earthquake destroyed their homes
- **C.** They were looking for better jobs

3. What part of the world does falafel come from?

- **A.** China
- **B.** Brazil
- **C.** Middle East

Find the answers at the back of the book.

25

STAYING CONNECTED

Our world is connected like never before. We're able to video chat with people in other countries. We share music, photos, and videos with the tap of a screen. Planes, trains, and cars whisk us from city to city and country to country. But it wasn't always this way.

Before motorized vehicles, travel took a long time. People had to walk, ride horses, or go by boat. When the explorer Christopher Columbus sailed to the Americas in 1492, it took him 10 weeks! Handwritten letters took just as long to reach their destination. But communication and travel started to speed up in the 1800s. Telegraphs and telephones delivered messages more quickly. Railroads crisscrossed the land, and steam-powered ships slashed travel times.

THE INTERNET AGE

The first electronic, programmable computers were invented in the 1940s. Although these early computers were the size of a room, they were puny in terms of computing power. And they couldn't "talk" to each other. Today's computers are small but powerful, and they're connected by the Internet.

THE BIRTH OF THE INTERNET

In the 1960s, engineers developed a secure way of sending packets of information from one computer to another. Small numbers of government computers shared information this way. In 1989, Tim Berners-Lee came up with the World Wide Web. This was a global "web" of information that anyone could access.

A MODEM ALLOWS A COMPUTER TO CONNECT TO AN INTERNET SERVICE PROVIDER (ISP).

WHEN YOU TYPE IN A URL (INTERNET ADDRESS), YOUR COMPUTER SENDS A REQUEST FOR THAT WEB PAGE. THE WEBSITE ARRIVES WITHIN SECONDS, EVEN IF THE FILES FOR IT ARE STORED ON THE OTHER SIDE OF THE WORLD.

SATELLITES IN ORBIT ABOVE EARTH SEND AND RECEIVE WIRELESS SIGNALS.

UNDERWATER CABLES CARRY SIGNALS FROM ONE CONTINENT TO ANOTHER.

THE DATA AND CODE THAT POWER WEBSITES ARE STORED ON VAST SERVER FARMS THAT ARE CONNECTED BY CABLES TO THE INTERNET.

SMARTPHONES CONNECT TO THE INTERNET USING WIRELESS TECHNOLOGY TO SEND AND RECEIVE INFORMATION VIA CELL PHONE TOWERS.

SIGNALS TRAVEL AT INCREDIBLE SPEEDS THROUGH COPPER OR FIBER-OPTIC CABLES.

AN ISP USES SERVERS TO DIRECT INFORMATION GOING BACK AND FORTH BETWEEN COMPUTERS AND THE INTERNET.

MOVING FASTER, MOVING FARTHER

Not all that long ago, travel was much less common than it is today. Only the rich could afford to go on long trips, and many people never traveled more than a short distance from the place where they were born. But now we're moving faster and farther than ever before.

THE AGE OF STEAM

Introduced in the 1830s, steam trains revolutionized travel. Passengers could easily go from one city to another, and from cities to the countryside. Goods could be transported more quickly, and newspapers and mail could travel faster, too.

GOING BY SEA

Of course, trains couldn't travel across the ocean, so traveling to Europe or Asia from the Americas still meant a long voyage by boat. By 1900, even the most modern ocean liners took almost a week to make the journey from New York to Britain. There were luxurious cabins for first-class passengers, but accommodation for the poor was cramped and very basic.

GETTING AROUND

Ocean liners and steam trains have been replaced with faster and more efficient forms of transportation. This is how people get around now:

CARS

Today there are more than one billion passenger cars on the world's roads, and that number is rising.

TRAINS

Powered by diesel or electricity, the fastest trains can travel at more than 250 mph (400 kmh). Subway trains carry passengers below busy cities.

AIRPLANES

Flying is the fastest way to travel between countries and continents. Every year there are almost 5 billion passenger journeys by plane.

THE FUTURE OF TRAVEL

What will travel look like in the future? It may be rather different:

SELF-DRIVING CARS

No driver required! Just tap to choose your destination, and the car's computer does the rest.

PASSENGER DRONES

Like self-driving cars, these flying taxis wouldn't need a driver, either.

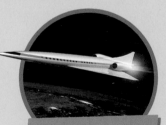

SPACE PLANES

By flying at the edge of space, hypersonic airliners would slash travel times.

SEEING THE WORLD

Traveling provides the opportunity to see exciting cities and Earth's natural wonders. It's a great way to meet people and explore new cultures. Tourism is increasingly popular—and it's big business, too.

ADVANTAGES OF TOURISM

Tourism can be a force for good. Here are a few of its positive sides:

BOOSTING THE ECONOMY

Tourists support local economies in the places that they visit. Hotels, shops, and local attractions depend on tourism.

SHARING CULTURES

People who visit another country often learn about the local culture.

PRESERVING SITES

If tourists come to see historic sites, local authorities are encouraged to preserve them.

MENTAL BOOST

Studies have shown that traveling reduces stress and boosts happiness, and it can increase your creativity.

DOWNSIDES OF TOURISM

Unfortunately, not all of the effects of tourism are positive. Here are some of the downsides:

RAISING EMISSIONS

Airplanes and other forms of transportation pollute the air with carbon dioxide, which contributes to climate change.

OVERCROWDING

Popular sites can become overrun with tourists and the litter they leave, spoiling their beauty and damaging their fragile ecosystems.

NO ROOM FOR LOCALS

In popular destinations, homes are turned into short-term rentals. This often pushes rents and property prices up, forcing local people out.

DAMAGING SITES

Developing locations often means building roads and other features that damage the natural environment.

THE FUTURE OF TOURISM?

Some companies want to take tourists to space! They're developing aircraft that can take passengers high enough to experience weightlessness— but at a price. One company is charging more than $200,000 for a short flight. Other companies want to take tourists to the Moon!

Not everyone on our planet is connected. Some people prefer to live a more secluded life, sticking to one location or community. In fact, some groups take this concept even further. They try to avoid all contact with the outside world.

REMOTE COMMUNITIES

We often call these groups "uncontacted tribes." They usually live in remote areas, such as the depths of the Amazon rain forest. They live off the land, building homes and making tools from the natural materials around them. Most of these groups live in harmony with nature in more or less the same way as their ancestors did.

SHRINKING NUMBERS

When Europeans started exploring the world centuries ago, it was not uncommon to find tribes who had never seen a white person before. Now uncontacted tribes are extremely rare. Scientists estimate that not many more than 100 of them remain, mostly in South America.

TRIBES AT RISK

Many of the world's uncontacted tribes stay hidden out of fear. In most cases, contact they've had with the outside world has ended badly for them. Tribes in South America learned to fear white Europeans, and that has been passed down to current generations.

Today there are real threats to tribes in the Amazon from people who want their land for ranching or logging. Some countries in the region have government departments whose job is to protect these tribes—while keeping their distance.

TOTALLY TRUE - OR - FOOLISHLY FALSE?

A. Uncontacted tribes have no idea that the outside world even exists.

B. People in uncontacted tribes have little immunity to common illnesses, which puts them at risk.

Find the answers at the back of the book.

IS IT BETTER TO BE CONNECTED?

Our world is connected in ways that previous generations could only dream of. Thanks to improvements in transportation and the rise of the Internet and social media, we are closer than ever before. But is that always a good thing?

THINK ABOUT IT!

? We can post messages on Internet sites without using our real names. Some people love this, but does it make people more likely to be mean and bully others?

? Social media allows us to share news and videos quickly, but how can we avoid being taken in by "fake news"?

? Travel is fast and cheap, but it contributes to climate change. Can you think of ways to travel more responsibly?

? People move around the world for many reasons, making it possible for illnesses such as Covid-19 to spread quickly. Should we travel less to stay safe?

HISTORY DETECTIVE

Find a screenshot of the world's first web page. How does it look different from today's websites?

TRAVEL CHAMP

Plan a route around the world using as many different forms of transportation as you can. How long would it take?

ROCKET-POWERED AIRSHIP

Thread a long piece of string through a straw, then tie one end to a doorknob and the other end to a chair, pulling the string tight.

Blow up a balloon and hold the end carefully to keep the air inside. Tape the balloon to the straw, let go, and watch your airship zoom off!

HOW CONNECTED ARE YOU?

Test your knowledge . . .

1. How long did it take Columbus to reach the Americas?

- **A.** 10 days
- **B.** 10 weeks
- **C.** 10 years

2. What role do satellites play in the Internet?

- **A.** Send and receive signals
- **B.** Look out for hackers
- **C.** Store website data

3. Approximately how many airline passenger journeys are made in an average year?

- **A.** 3 billion
- **B.** 4 billion
- **C.** 5 billion

Find the answers at the back of the book.

WHAT IS GLOBALIZATION?

There's a word for the way in which our modern world is becoming more connected: globalization. It's more than just traveling the world and sharing videos over the Internet. Globalization is about the world's countries and economies becoming more closely linked.

Is there a McDonald's or a Starbucks near where you live? Travel around the world, and you may well find another one! Both these companies started in the United States, but now they operate in many different countries. These are just two examples of businesses that have expanded around the world. Modern transportation and communication have made it possible for companies and brands to do business almost anywhere they like.

FOOD MILES

When was the last time you ate a banana? Chances are it traveled thousands of miles to reach you. Our ancestors had to make do with whatever food they could grow locally, eating only what was in season. Now we can feast on foods from around the world at any time of year.

HOW FAR?

Even a simple meal can use ingredients from all over the world. Today food can be shipped from anywhere in the world, moving quickly enough to arrive before it spoils. Food travels by boat, plane, train, and truck, but all these forms of delivery release carbon dioxide, which causes climate change. People sometimes talk about "food miles," which is a simple way of expressing how far your food has traveled to end up on your plate. Local food is often better for the environment. Imagine that you are eating a pizza and a smoothie in Britain. See where all the ingredients have traveled from.

OLIVES FROM SPAIN

PEPPERONI MADE IN AN ITALIAN FACTORY, USING PORK FROM PIGS RAISED IN GERMANY

PIZZA BASE USES FLOUR MADE FROM WHEAT GROWN IN IRELAND

CHEESE MADE FROM THE MILK OF COWS RAISED IN THE UK

TOMATOES FROM ITALY, MADE INTO SAUCE AT A FACTORY IN FRANCE

YOGURT FROM GREECE, TRANSPORTED ON A REFRIGERATED TRUCK

YOGHURT

BLUEBERRIES FROM MOROCCO, TRANSPORTED BY PLANE

GROUND BLACK PEPPER FROM VIETNAM, TRANSPORTED BY SHIP

BANANAS FROM COLOMBIA, SHIPPED ACROSS THE OCEAN

STRAWBERRIES GROWN IN A GREENHOUSE IN THE NETHERLANDS AND SENT BY TRAIN

JOBS IN A GLOBAL ECONOMY

Globalization has changed the way we live, and it's changing the way we work, too. In the past, a company hiring workers had to make do with the people in the local area. Now large companies can set up factories and call centers on the opposite side of the globe and hire workers from anywhere.

MULTINATIONAL CORPORATIONS

In the past, although a small number of traders traveled long distances to find exotic goods, most businesses bought and sold within their local community. Now large companies have branches in many countries. An organization might have its headquarters in one country but also own factories and sales offices in many other countries.

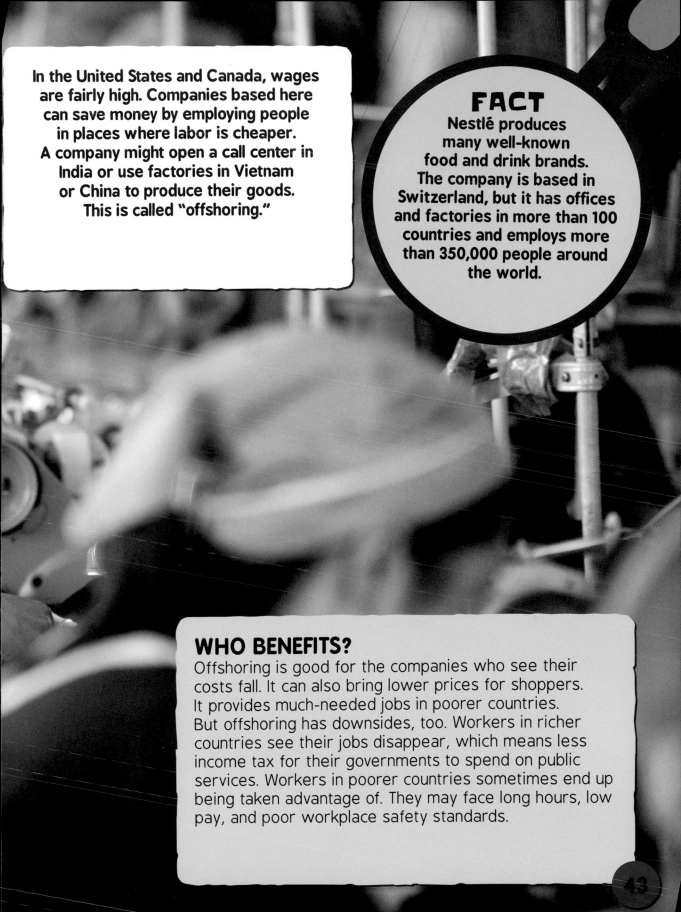

In the United States and Canada, wages are fairly high. Companies based here can save money by employing people in places where labor is cheaper. A company might open a call center in India or use factories in Vietnam or China to produce their goods. This is called "offshoring."

FACT

Nestlé produces many well-known food and drink brands. The company is based in Switzerland, but it has offices and factories in more than 100 countries and employs more than 350,000 people around the world.

WHO BENEFITS?

Offshoring is good for the companies who see their costs fall. It can also bring lower prices for shoppers. It provides much-needed jobs in poorer countries. But offshoring has downsides, too. Workers in richer countries see their jobs disappear, which means less income tax for their governments to spend on public services. Workers in poorer countries sometimes end up being taken advantage of. They may face long hours, low pay, and poor workplace safety standards.

THE WORLD'S FACTORIES

Have you ever read the small print on the tag in your jeans? How about the back of your phone or tablet? It should say where the product was made. And there's a good chance it won't be where you live. Many of the goods we use today are manufactured overseas.

WI-FI CHIP DESIGNED BY AN AMERICAN COMPANY AND MADE IN MEXICO

Many popular brands of smartphones are assembled in China. However, the workers there are putting together parts that can come from all over the world. Smartphones are truly global products!

AUDIO CHIP DESIGNED BY AN AMERICAN COMPANY AND MADE IN SINGAPORE

FACT
Some countries specialize in making specific kinds of products. Many well-known clothing brands have their garments sewn in India, Vietnam, or Bangladesh.

AND THE WINNER IS . . .
China is often called "the factory of the world" because so many goods are manufactured there. In fact, 20 percent of all global manufacturing takes place in China. The United States is in second place, with 18 percent, and Japan is third.

CAMERA AND MEMORY CHIP FROM JAPAN

ACCELEROMETER (A TYPE OF MOTION SENSOR) DESIGNED BY A GERMAN COMPANY

BATTERY FROM SOUTH KOREA

LCD SCREEN DESIGNED BY A SOUTH KOREAN COMPANY BUT MANUFACTURED IN POLAND

GLASS SCREEN DESIGNED BY AN AMERICAN COMPANY AND MADE IN MALAYSIA

WHY GO OVERSEAS?

Cheap labor is a significant reason why companies choose factories in other parts of the world. Some countries, including China, also offer tax breaks to attract manufacturers. Strict environmental laws and health and safety rules in the US and Canada can also make manufacturing more expensive. It's cheaper to make goods in places where these laws don't apply.

LOCAL OR GLOBAL?

Every day we eat food from around the world and use products made in faraway factories. But there are usually farms and factories in our local area, too. Should we all be trying to buy local?

THINK ABOUT IT!

? You don't have to worry about food miles when buying food from local producers, but you probably won't find pineapples or coffee at the local farmers market. Why do you think this is?

? Grocery stores buy huge amounts of food from large companies. Do you think this makes it hard for small local producers to get their food on the shelves?

? If goods are manufactured locally instead of in cheaper places, they might cost more. Do you think people would be willing to pay more if it meant more jobs for local people, with good wages and working conditions?

? Many of the products manufactured in the developing world are designed and sold by companies in richer countries. Who do you think benefits most from this arrangement?

BE A LOCAVORE

Visit a farmers market to see what foods are available from your local suppliers, then plan and cook a local meal for your family.

LABEL DETECTIVE

Look for labels on your clothes and other products to see where they are made, then find those countries on a map.

FOOD-MILES MATH

Check the labels to find out where your food was produced. How far has each ingredient traveled? Which came from farthest away?

ARE YOU A GLOBAL GENIUS?

Test your knowledge . . .

1. Which gas is released when food is shipped overseas?

A. carbon dioxide

B. nitrous oxide

C. helium

2. What is it called when a company hires workers in a different country?

A. outdistancing

B. overcompensating

C. offshoring

3. Which country produces more manufactured goods than any other?

A. China

B. United States

C. Bangladesh

Find the answers at the back of the book.

SOLVING PROBLEMS

In our modern world we face many problems—everything from unemployment and pollution to pandemics and climate change. Some of these problems can be solved locally. Others require the cooperation of people and governments all over the world.

Companies and cultures no longer exist in a single country. Neither do some of the problems we face! Pollution created in one country can drift into another. Carbon dioxide emitted in one part of the world affects the climate in other parts. Often, trash from one country is taken to a landfill in another.

Luckily, many of the people working to solve these problems aren't limited by borders either. Charities and other organizations bring together people from all over the globe to help tackle the world's biggest problems.

Countries make their own laws, but they often also cooperate with other countries. There are many different international organizations, each with its own list of member countries.

FIRST STEPS

When World War I ended in 1918, no one wanted to see another war on that scale again, so the League of Nations was set up to help solve disputes between countries. But many countries—including the United States—refused to join. They feared that being a member would drag them into international disputes.

THE UNITED NATIONS

The League of Nations was unable to prevent World War II (1939–1945). As a result of this second war, a new organization was set up: the United Nations (UN). The UN works to improve people's lives around the world. Almost all of the world's countries are now members. They send representatives to meet at the UN headquarters in New York City.

FACT

The UN has a team of interpreters who simultaneously translate between the six official languages of the UN so that members can understand all the debates.

UN AGENCIES

In order to address a wide range of issues, the UN has many different agencies. Here are just a few of them:

UNICEF

Provides children with vaccinations, education, clean water, and more.

THE WORLD BANK

Provides loans and grants to developing countries for projects such as creating schools or irrigation programs.

UNHCR

The United Nations High Commissioner for Refugees protects and cares for refugees.

FAO

The Food and Agriculture Organization aims to end world hunger and help farmers.

KEEPING IT LOCAL

The UN is a global group. Other international organizations are smaller and focus on regional issues:

EUROPEAN UNION

Citizens of its 27 member nations can live and work in any EU country.

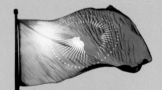

AFRICAN UNION

Aims to settle disputes between African nations and eliminate poverty.

ARAB LEAGUE

A group of Arabic-speaking countries in North Africa and the Middle East.

ASSOCIATION OF SOUTHEAST ASIAN NATIONS

Southeast Asian nations working to improve trade and promote peace.

NATURAL DISASTERS

Natural disasters can strike anywhere and at any time. Countries try to be prepared, but sometimes the unexpected happens. After an earthquake, tsunami, or hurricane, fast action is required to save lives. People from other countries often step in to help.

DISASTER ALERT!

A natural disaster is any crisis caused by Earth's natural processes, such as . . .

EARTHQUAKES

LANDSLIDES

VOLCANIC ERUPTIONS

TORNADOES

FLOODS

WILDFIRES

DROUGHTS

TSUNAMIS

METEOR IMPACTS

HURRICANES

FIRST RESPONSE

People are often injured or killed in natural disasters. Local emergency services spring into action. International workers often help, too. They rescue people trapped in collapsed buildings, set up emergency shelters, and treat the injured.

REBUILDING

Often the aftereffects of natural disasters can be just as dangerous as the events themselves. Disasters can destroy homes and buildings, knock out electricity, and damage clean water supplies. It takes a lot of work to get life back to normal.

RED CROSS, RED CRESCENT

The Red Cross was originally set up in Switzerland in 1863 to assist soldiers wounded in battle. Now it works to help anyone affected by war or natural disasters. Most countries have their own Red Cross society, though in Muslim countries they are called Red Crescent societies. These groups will help anyone in need, regardless of their nationality or religion.

TOTALLY TRUE - OR - FOOLISHLY FALSE?

A. The Indian Ocean tsunami of 2004 killed more than 225,000 people.

B. "Typhoon" and "hurricane" are different names for the same type of storm.

C. The Red Cross has won the Nobel Peace Prize twice for its work saving lives.

Find the answers at the back of the book.

PꙬNDEMIC PꙬNIC

Toward the end of 2019, a new virus spread around the world. In March 2020, the World Health Organization (WHO) declared that the new disease—called "Covid-19"—was a pandemic.

WHAT IS A PANDEMIC?

A pandemic is an outbreak of a disease that occurs over a wide area and affects a large number of people. Previous pandemics, such as the black death in the 1300s and the Spanish flu, which began in 1918, killed tens of millions of people around the world.

SPREADING FAST

Our connected modern world allows pandemics to spread more quickly than ever before. Many diseases, including Covid-19, spread particularly easily because people can infect others without even realizing they have it. If one of those people gets on a plane, the virus arrives in another country and starts a new chain of infection, which can spread rapidly. Within six months, Covid-19 had reached almost every country on Earth.

STOPPING THE SPREAD

Each country makes its own decisions on how to fight pandemics like Covid-19. Keeping people apart slows the spread of the infection, so in 2020 many countries went into "lockdown." People were required to stay at home as much as possible.

SCIENTISTS UNITE!

Scientists around the world share their knowledge to fight pandemics. They race to develop drugs to treat the disease and vaccines to prevent it. Doctors also cooperate to find the best way to treat patients with the disease. Even governments and health services can work together, sending equipment where it's needed most.

CLIMATE CHANGE

Earth is growing warmer, and humans are the cause. This rise in temperature is already starting to cause serious problems—which are affecting everyone on Earth. Climate change is probably the biggest challenge we face, and countries will need to work together like never before to stop it.

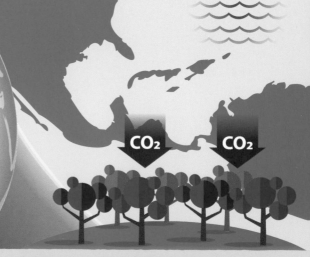

COWS AND OTHER LIVESTOCK RELEASE A GAS CALLED METHANE (CH_4) WHEN THEY BURP OR EXPEL GAS. METHANE TRAPS HEAT.

HIGHER TEMPERATURES CHANGE NORMAL WEATHER PATTERNS. SEVERE STORMS, FLOODING, HEAT WAVES, AND DROUGHTS ALL BECOME MORE COMMON.

WHEN THE WATER IN THE OCEANS HEATS UP, IT EXPANDS AND TAKES UP MORE SPACE. THIS MAKES SEA LEVELS RISE.

STOPPING CLIMATE CHANGE

The most important step for stopping climate change is to produce less carbon dioxide. This will require hard choices. We'll have to travel less and consume less. Governments will need to invest a lot of money in other types of energy, such as wind and solar power. We also need to help those whose lives are already being affected by climate change.

TREES TAKE IN CARBON DIOXIDE (CO_2) FROM THE AIR AND STORE IT. WHEN FORESTS ARE CUT DOWN, LESS CO_2 CAN BE ABSORBED.

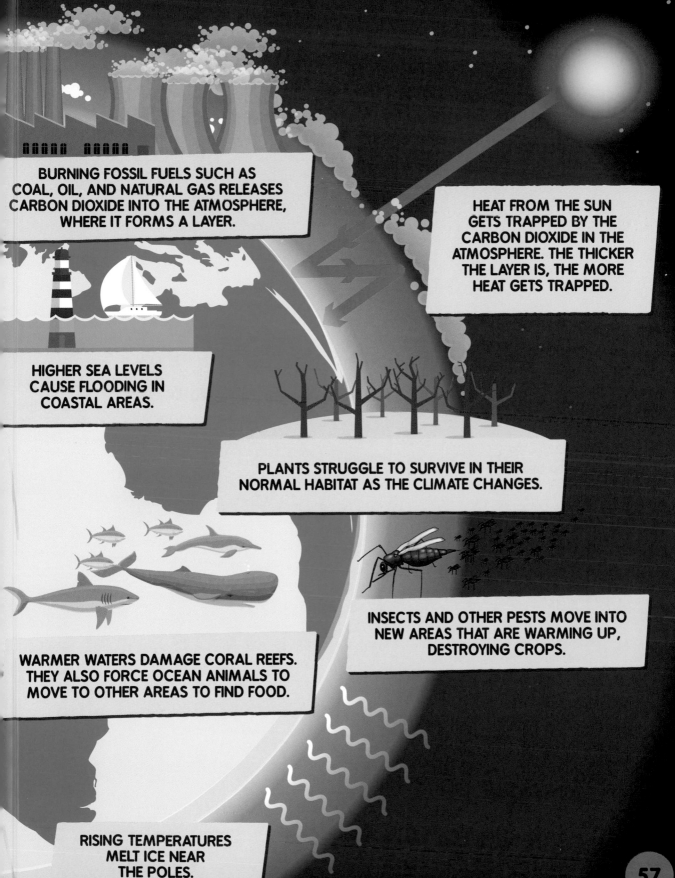

WHAT IF WE DON'T AGREE?

Different people have conflicting ideas about how to solve problems, and that goes for countries too! The most serious disputes can lead to war. Even smaller disagreements can affect our ability to deal with global problems like climate change.

THINK ABOUT IT!

? The UN tries to solve disagreements between countries. It also works to improve the lives of ordinary people. Do you think these roles are equally important?

? Some countries have made international agreements to try to reduce climate change. But not all countries sign up. Do you think it's fair that some countries make tough changes to stop climate change if others don't?

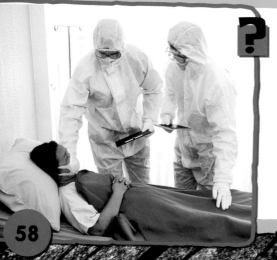

? A connected planet allowed Covid-19 to spread quickly, but it also allowed scientists to share their knowledge in the hope of beating it. How do you think the crisis might have been different if it had happened 200 years ago?

ACTIVITIES TO TRY

KNOW YOUR UN

Research some of the agencies of the UN. What do they do? Are there any that you would like to be a part of one day?

DISASTER HERO

Can you help a disaster-relief agency? They may need donations of everyday items such as clothing, food, or toiletries.

GREEN CHAMPION

Trees absorb carbon dioxide. Can you plant one at home or at school? Or could you get involved with a tree-planting program in your local area?

LOW-CARBON LIVING

How often do you travel in a car? How many of your trips could you replace with a more eco-friendly travel method like walking or biking?

ARE YOU A CHAMPION OF COOPERATION?

Test your knowledge . . .

1. When was the United Nations set up?

A. At the end of WWI

B. At the end of WWII

C. During the Covid-19 pandemic

2. What is the society that helps those affected by war or natural disaster called?

A. Red Cross

B. Blue Cross

C. Orange Crescent

3. What happens when seawater heats up?

A. It becomes more polluted

B. It reflects more sunlight

C. It expands and takes up more space

Find the answers at the back of the book.

A GREENER FUTURE

In our modern connected world, the way we live puts great strain on the planet and its resources. But we can tackle this problem by changing our lifestyles. We can also work to give all people around the world the same chance to be safe, healthy, and happy.

WHAT HAPPENS NEXT?

Earth's growing population creates big challenges. More people means more mouths to feed and more use of energy and natural resources. Scientists predict that population growth will slow down and almost stop by the year 2100, but we still need to use less per person to live sustainably. But don't people in the developing world also have a right to a better standard of living? It's a delicate balance.

FACT

We're already making changes. One example is the huge rise in electric cars, which don't release carbon dioxide. In 2012, there were hardly 100,000 electric cars on the road. Now there are more than 4 million, and the number is rising quickly.

I SPEAK FOR THE TREES FOR THE TREES HAVE NO TONGUES

— THE LORAX